Upon Your Canvas

Upon Your Canvas

Paul Goldman, MS

Paintings by Natosha Keefer

Upon Your Canvas
Copyright © 2015 by Paul Goldman
www.ecstaticpoet.com

All rights reserved. No part of this book may be reproduced in any form or by any electronic or mechanical means including information storage and retrieval systems, without permission in writing from the authors.

Book interior and cover design by River Sanctuary Graphic Arts

ISBN (Print version) 978-1-935914-50-1
ISBN (e-Book version) 978-1-935914-54-9

Printed in the United States of America

Additional copies available from:
www.ecstaticpoet.com

Library of Congress Control Number: 2015931133

River Sanctuary Publishing
P.O. Box 1561
Felton, California 95018

www.riversanctuarypublishing.com

Dedicated to the awakening of the New Earth

For Dawn

my beloved wife

Imagine in this moment, you yourself are a blank canvas. Trust at depth the knowledge innate within your own bones:

> *... that you are filled with the freedom to create your own color palette.*

Whatever you dream, is available for you.
You decide this time how your life is to manifest.

So, come on in and paint YOU any way you see fit.
All of you is more than welcome here.

Come on in, come on in…

Namaste,

Paul

Poems

I. At First Brush

Upon Your Canvas 1
And There Is One Thing 2
Eyes That Matter 3
True Wealth's Secret 4
What Is It That You Want To Know? 5
Golden Like A Leaf 6
Falling Into A Flower 7
My Dearest Vincent 8
Holy Instant of Change 10
Evolution Revolution 11

II. Light and Shadow

Rushing Not 15
The Promise 16
Twice 17
Have You Ever 18
Live Simply 19
Snapped The Cycle 20
Cloud Signs 21
I Bow 22

III. Canvas Revelation

Purple Sky 25
By Your Still Waters 26
Amygdala Leave Me Alone 28
Is There Yet More? 29
Bringing You 30

We Are All Gems	31
Reaching Out	32
The Fourth, The Fifth, The Minor Fall, The Major Lift	34
Set Free	36
Arise	37
Believe Anything	38
I Am Who You Are	39
Elk's Selfless Gift	40
Secret Chambers	41
You Have Got A Right To Know	42
Two Lefts Make A Right	44
Spellbound Leap	45
Notes of Bliss	46
Lotus of Becoming	47
Deeper	48
The Gift of Brush	50
Sensing Beyond Sensing	51
Come Home, Come Home	52
I See	53
The Sweeping Sands	54
Magnificence Realized	55
Flowers of Awakening	56
Completely Out of My Mind	57
Dancing in The Shift	58
This Reverent Madness	60
Syncopation	61
Love (at last) Entered	63
About the Author	64
About the Artist	65
Paintings by Natosha Keefer	66

I.

At First Brush

Upon Your Canvas

Upon your canvas, I am laid bare.
You reveal all the colors,
that comprise my being.

I am awash in hues of
purple, indigo and forest green,

a chiaroscuro whisper of light—
stroked by the delicate brush— of your
hand Divine.

And There Is One Thing

I turned to go, just as She
called out to say there
is just one thing you ought
to know.

Now, my curiosity was way up.

I had to know what this one thing
was.

The wait was as short as Her word,
just the one word, followed me
into the rest of the day:

presence.

Eyes That Matter

In the eyes of the One
who sees, I have come
no farther than I always

have been. In my eyes,
these new lenses see
every single thing

for the first time, even
the one I had come to know
as myself, is viewed as if revealed

only in this moment.

To see through eyes
that matter, is sweet relief.

True Wealth's Secret

Tonight, I saw You
once more and knew
beyond, beneath, within,
without – that I am.

The resonant beauty
of everything shimmers—
in this vast field of being.

Tonight, I found true wealth's
secret and vowed to keep
You – forever sacred.

What Is It That You Want To Know?

Beneath the surface of silence, the still question
is asked and answered.

And yet, the refrain is louder still – asking,
"Yes, and what is it that you want to know?"

Again, beneath the surface of silence, the still
question is asked and answered.

Once more, the echoes of "what is it that you want to know?"
reverberate…"what is it that you want to know?",
"what is it that you want to know?"

Golden Like A Leaf

The sheer sight of you is golden,
like an autumn leaf falling, falling
free in the gentle breeze.

I stand to watch mesmerized at
each moment, as you— like a leaf,
separate from branch after branch,

to begin your

free-fall.

Your laughter fills the skies
as your reverie rivals even
the golden leaf in boundless

flight.

Falling Into A Flower

With each breath, I fall
deeper into the flower
that is you.

To sit and separate your
bloom, petal by petal
is to know the magnificent

detail put into place,
simply for each of us
to experience.

Scent, texture, complexity,
all startle me alive
in the moment of you,

as I fall deeper and deeper
      into a flower.

My Dearest Vincent

I received your sweet gift
yesterday, tattered linen
a palette of bloodstain and oil paint.

Your brushstrokes were gallant—
I recognized your hand at once,

I do know why you slashed
your ear, for me,

after all these years, the voices
that drove you to such a delightful
madness into The Starry Night

still speak, I lay your angelic ear
on my pillow at night,
at first their roar disturbed me
now I cannot wait each evening

to lay beside, to hear—
their inspiration amazes,
I am creative beyond
my wildest desires,

though, I must admit
my increasing madness
shocks a number of our
old friends,

their clamor is forever
drowned out,
as I find more time
to rest my ear
beside yours,

My Dearest Vincent,
madness, Divine madness—
the sweetest gift...

Holy Instant of Change

We who are alive
in the crisp realization
of this moment,
seek to bring
recognition
of the One,

a keen knowing
of connection one
to another.

Now is our
time, our time
to be so alive!

When everything
manifests
at once,
in this holy—

instant of change.

Evolution Revolution

Each breath is evolution,
a peaceful revolution
of our own being.

We evolve as
we inhale,
exhale,

we evolve
in each awakened
realization.

We who have
embarked
here now,

are all spiritual warriors,
engaged in this evolution
revolution.

II.

Light and Shadow

Rushing Not

Rushing not to judgment,
only observing phenomena.

Becoming the witness
to self and others,
one and the same.

Seeing beyond vision's
gift, into allowing
events to unfold

–of their own accord–

rushing not to judgment,
observing phenomena,
becoming the witness…

The Promise

To see beyond
that which we
have seen before;

to even sense new
synapses firing
for the very first time,

in remembrance of
our soul's desire,
this, *this* is the promise

or our lifetime.

Twice

Believe if you will in the happenstance
of singular sensation, just random events
with no quantum intersect.

I choose to find the coincidence
of events merging and colliding

into the realm of twice, worth recognizing.

For in these duels of doubles, patterns
begin to emerge, stories unfold
with a definite plot.

We are not given a glance just to skip ahead—
ignoring beginning, middle and end.
Rather, precisely when the twice moments arise,

we are indeed given the oft referenced second chance
to rewrite not only how our particular story
develops, red herrings and all,

but even how this one is going to *end*.

Have You Ever

Have you ever wondered
how you got here?
And then in the next
breath, realized that here

is exactly where you have been
all of your life. Seems kind of funny
to come to the reckoning that

what has been so long searched
for, has always been here,
right here in the midst of this.

Here is here. There is not even
a there— there or here. Only this
being here, present to each breath,

each miracle of moment,
happening in only one place,
   here, right here, right now.

Live Simply

From the depths of memory,
flood these feelings of familiarity,
and a deep knowing that

we have been this way,
so many times before.

That is why when we simply
allow ourselves to live
simply, we find it so easy

to simply live.

Snapped The Cycle

Each of us IS
arisen anew
day by day,
moment by moment,
the words LACK,
FEAR, NOT ENOUGH,
flash across the neon sky,
yet we too know
this is the ILLUSION.

The task then is
to release the grip
we have placed upon
ourselves and let go,
and let go, and let go—
until without a doubt
we have snapped the
cycle of disbelief.

Then, we feel our own breath
[with every fiber of our being]
and know we have come

back to the center of
not only our own selves,

yet the very essence of
everything that is HOLY!

Cloud Signs

Everywhere she looks within the painted sky,
she sees the signs in clouds, across the horizon,
stroked into being by the unseen brush.

Here a dragon comes to life, there the face
and wings of an angel. A few sweeps to the east,
a buffalo snorts, sniffs and taps just one hoof to ancient prairie.

As her own inner eyes have awakened amidst the silence
indwelling, her outer eyes— as if their very anatomical functioning
had changed— now see revealed amongst the wisps

and whispers painted from a palette divine,
messages of hope, of wonder and of a certain salvation
whose time is here.

I will not be surprised if soon she does not begin to see
beyond these images, mythic or real, to ask me:
do you see the words scripted across the sky?

I Bow

With such gratitude
for each thing,
quite profound
or even mundane,

that fills the field
of my existence,
I bow to the One

who carries me
always and in
so many ways

that I have yet,
to even imagine…

III.
Canvas Revelation

Purple Sky

Barely having scratched
the surface of our own
creativity,

today we paint
a new landscape—

with purple sky,
and our flag
of revealed possibility,

unfurled!

By Your Still Waters

By Your still waters,
I fall deeper and deeper,
into that which I am becoming.

No longer content with what was,
settling silently into the Self
that directs and orchestrates

a symphonic peace in my life.

By Your still waters,
I fall deeper and deeper,
ever deeper…

Amygdala Leave Me Alone

In each moment, I have
a choice to react
from my amygdala,

knowing that there is indeed
a saber tooth tiger
charging, ready to devour,

or let loose both barrels of reason
and see the perceived threat
as merely what it is—

an information source.

To access the golden
fruit contained,

I need only allow my pause
button to engage, for herein lies

the gift of self responsibility,
and the subtle
ability to speak words

that heal, instead of wound.

Is There Yet More?

Swirling, whirling with all
you have freely given me,
I ask is there yet more?

And to hear the answer
that there is even more
to come, swells my heart

with a passion to live
I have never felt before.

This knowing there is
even yet more and more,
is beyond imagining,

  beyond breathing itself,
    beyond this blissful moment,
      beyond, even beyond…

Bringing You

Bringing You into
the very structure of my DNA,
manifests change— wrought at

a quantum molecular level.

Is it any wonder, I have
become a ship sailing
on the seas of shift?

Clouds pass by so often,
that I have grown accustomed
to them appearing, reappearing—

Buddha's face one instant,
Mary the next. Krishna here,
Kuan Yin now.

Intertwined in this wrapping,
rewrapping, whole new strands
have emerged, which even

now I am lost in the unconscious

integration; bringing You,
me, every single thing
into a singular state

of being…

We Are All Gems

There comes a time when
we see our own reflection,
maybe in the passing image

in another's eyes, or if we
are extremely lucky— glancing
back at ourselves from a mirror.

At these moments the raw,
uncut, unfaceted parts of each
one of us so sparkles,

that we cannot keep from
being amazed at the light,
the pure light, that shimmers

from, around and through us.
We see now what has been
ever present— the gift

of our own magnificence,
the most precious gem—
now realized.

Reaching Out

Reaching out to you,
I reach back to me.

Arms that enfold you
are not only my arms,
they are the very same

arms of the Beloved.
What if in reaching out
one to another, we were

to become aware of just
whose arms so intertwine us?
There would be a celebration

of ceaseless reaching out,
one to another, arms
enfolding each other,

arms enfolding the globe.
Picture that, just picture that!

The Fourth, The Fifth, The Minor Fall, The Major Lift

I've heard there was a secret chord
That David played, and it please the Lord
But you don't care for music, do you?
It goes like this
The fourth, the fifth,
the minor fall, the major lift
The baffled king composing Hallelujah

Hallelujah, Hallelujah
Hallelujah, Hallelujah…
    ~Leonard Cohen

Yes, I have come to you
to sing, to only sing
Hallelujah, Hallelujah!

For, I too have seen the Lord
and he says to tell you hello,
to ask how you are?

Hallelujah, Hallelujah!

Yes, I have experienced the fourth,
the fifth, the minor fall and the
heavenly major lift.

Hallelujah, Hallelujah!

Of them all, I do not so much
remember the fourth or the fifth—
and only too well recall the minor fall.

Hallelujah, Hallelujah!

I am here to tell you the major lift
is real, so real. The time comes
when there is nothing left,

the only way to go is up, grab
on for the major lift—

ride your fourth, your fifth
and even your minor fall,
for surely comes your major lift!

Hallelujah, Hallelujah!
Hallelujah, Hallelujah!

Set Free

Set free,
we fly,
on angel's wings.

Set free, we sing
songs our heart
has never heard.

Set free, we find
our self, the one
we have been
longing for,

the one who
has been
right here,
ever present,

and available,
the one who
has always,
already— set us free…

Arise

Arise!
   Arise!
      Arise!

That is all
you or I need
to do.

Nothing else,

just simply
Arise!
   Arise!
      Arise!

Believe Anything

Believe anything!

Hear the voice now
and listen, listen as if
your own life depended

upon these ecstatic sounds
reaching deep into you,
setting your ears to dancing

in the sound of twilight.

Listen, listen as if your
eyes cannot believe
the sight of that which

your ears hear. Know that
really, at last, there are no bounds
to what you can accomplish!

Yes, believe anything,
believe beneath the
woven fabric of your being,

believe anything is possible,
even that which you desire most.

Believe anything and *everything*,
is yet possible, even beyond that…

I Am Who You Are

I am who you are. I am here
to both reveal
and be revealed.

In you lay me, in the depths
of me, lie you.

We swim in the same ocean
of longing, of love, of absolute
rapture;

synchronized stroke by precious stroke,
even yet now breath by breath—
  you are who I am… who I am,
    you are.

Elk's Selfless Gift

Beloved elk, your selfless gift
of your own rich hide,
leaves me bereft of words

to express my deep gratitude.
For now, your speckled damp skin
nuzzles around the fifteen inch hoop

drum, drying. In my vision,
you have spoken to me.

This drum still being birthed
is an ancestor drum, here
at this beat between beats

to share wisdom, to teach
through the drum skin speak
about our wondrous relationships,

about our chance to learn from the Creator
about ourselves, each other
and our boundless connection

to our Earth Mother— yet rocking
us now in her cradle to the beat
of your endless gift…

Secret Chambers

What must I do
to pluck the eternal
strings of your heart?

Is there yet a melody
that only you
long for?

Teach me the notes
to play, so that I
can enter the secret

chambers of your heart.
Let me in and invite me
to dance with you,

there in the quiet dark,
where no one else
has been.

You Have Got A Right To Know

Here is what I have been told:
there is so much more to all of this,
than meets our wandering eye.

Set before us is a bounty unlike
anything we think we have ever seen.

Rumors of lack have pelted the planet
far too long, as forbearers of doom,
have spread the ominous threat of lack, like wildfire.

Sure as each sunrise
and setting sun, there is no more
falsehood that has borne such fruit.

In an instant, the planetary switch
can be pulled, letting loose a gilded
array of plenty for every man, woman and child,

to live in perfect health, peace, harmony
and prosperity. It is up to each one of us
to SEE with renewed vision,

and a consciousness raised
sufficient to recognize that we indeed rise
or fall as ONE people,

in service to one another.

About all of this, you have, after all,
got a right to know.

Two Lefts Make A Right

For you, I dance ecstatic.
You do not seem to mind
my lack of rhythm or

that I am, in fact, dancing
with two left feet.

Quite the contrary, as tonight
you tell me that
these two left feet

whirling and spinning,
sliding and gliding around you,
are just right.

Spellbound Leap

To leap spellbound
into our life as if
there was no

as if at all,

is to know
we have already
arrived and the door
is wide open,

to our soul's
longing desire.

Notes of Bliss

At once the proverbial
light bulb goes on!

With the sheer intensity
of new light revealed, there is only
this instant of awakening

that really matters.

Every important thing
going on, is revealed
to be just another
thing going on,

not good, not bad—
just more experience
unembellished.

Feel your breath celebrate,
 in, out, in simple symphonic notes,
of bliss, in and out, in and out…

Lotus of Becoming

I am the thousand petals
of a golden lotus, flowering
even now into that

which I am becoming. Each new
opening revealing causality, hidden
away until this time.

Root by root, I am tapping into
the fertile Source of my own being.

This one I am becoming is not
unlike what I had envisioned
before this time of flesh and bone.

This must be why who I am
beneath these barriers of tight buds,
is so rich and familiar.

I see you too, ever opening
to the lotus, you are
becoming.

Deeper

This morning, we tiptoe
into the river of breath,
allowing each inhale,
exhale to take us deeper,

ever deeper than before.
Here, there is no shallow,
no surface— only going deeper

into our own ocean, an inner
world rich, expansive and
unceasing in its constant revelations,

of You, as we go even deeper still…

The Gift of Brush
(For Karen and For Natosha)

Within your soft brushstrokes
are revealed the same One
who sets these words to page.

It is in that common intersect
of art and poetry, where we
each listen, deeply listen

to the Voice, that never guides
us into places we are not ready
to go. You command paint

to appear as your inner vision
sees. I apply these words
to the blank page, praying

that each of them can even
come close to conveying
what my heart hears.

We each are grateful recipients
of this gift of brush, allowing
our own palette to display colors—

unseen until now.

Sensing Beyond Sensing

to have the gift of sight,
yet to see more than
eyes see, to hear more
than ears hear, to feel
this bliss more than
a heart can feel,
to be overflowing
with and in You!,
to be alive
in this space
of constant Grace,
miracles are indeed
the sum, of what we *are*.

Come Home, Come Home

Ripples of time, skip pebbles
across my heart, as the letting go
gets easier.

Past and future no longer
have any meaning.

In the bliss of silent memory,
we just listen— to the sound—
calling us, calling us
home…

I See

With eyes closed, I see beyond
the initial impression
of what is going on.

Beneath the surface of intent,
all is awash in a constant sea
of mass potentiality.

What is bubbling up is
not an eruption of volcanic
debris, rather there is only

this sweet hiss of release.
Your words sail away
and back again.

I see all around me
with eyes yet closed—
as far as the sky can reach

in all directions, I see…

The Sweeping Sands

I hear the sound
of the sweeping sands,
as the shift is quickening.

Right beneath our very feet,
time itself is both at a standstill
in serene moments and ever rushing
faster and faster forward

into a future certain to bring
us, into a grand connective
of One people, One Love,

One unfoldment in perfect
Bliss… listen to the sound
of the sweeping sands
     surrounding us.

Magnificence Realized

The shimmer of something
familiar greeted my eyes
this morning, as if I had

been waiting for a sign,
for a reminder of what I knew
to be the truth.

Nothing of wonder had in reality
faded from view.

I had only averted my eyes,
for a blip of moment,

from this immeasurable
magnificence yet realized
before me. Awe returned—

as if this feeling could ever
really vanish, from each breath.
And my breath, oh my breath and the next…

Flowers of Awakening

All day the scent of
Your flowers of awakening
has left me enraptured.

Wherever I turn, there is
this unmistakable indescribable
essence of wonder enveloping all of me.

Now, I desire only to remain
captured by Your aromatic
design, content to thrive

in this holy garden, where
the flowers of awakening—
always grow.

Completely Out of My Mind

Okay, I will say it out loud,
today I am completely out of my mind!
And this just feels so good to be finally

out of my mind, uncontained, prancing
like a filly who has just found legs
and hooves for the first time. This freedom

of movement, in this formerly hoarder's bedroom,
now expansive, resplendent with emptiness,
cannot be adequately described in mere words.

I invite you to do everything and nothing simultaneously
to find your own path to losing your mind. Who needs
one anyway?

Come, come play with me in this fertile field of no mind!
We can be free like we never thought before as there
are no thoughts, no judgments to mar the landscape.

Come now and completely lose your mind.
Think, if you can, of the fun we will have…

Dancing in The Shift

Today, each one of us
is dancing in the shift.
We have begun to learn

the sublime rhythm of paradox.
Everything has changed, whole
parts of ourselves have faded away—

along with past and future, yet we
remain the person we have always
been, now unencumbered by STUFF!

With this new found freedom, the melodies
ring out from our new encoded DNA.

Dancing in the shift is our neurobiological
imperative, as if our very molecular cells
themselves are dancing and they are.

You will need no encouragement once
this happens with your own being.

yet I must shout from all the rooftops:
the time is now to join this ecstatic dance
in the shift, so get your whole awakened self

shaking now, and dance, dance, dance…

This Reverent Madness

This madness has settled
over the alabaster landscape
once more. All of my friends

have gone Van Gogh, and cut off
just the one ear.

Now, mind you, this has not been
done in haste. It was just that this
constant ringing of love bells,

drove them to it. You see, the human
ear can only hear so much love.

And then every quantum action
requires the requisite reaction.
So, when you see the bandages

caressing these lovers' heads,
do not mourn for them. Just listen
ever more deeply to the sounds of love,
ever resounding…

Syncopation

Wholly new rhythms beat
an ecstatic pulse
beneath the firing

and misfiring
of my own desire.

I come before You
this day to discover
new layers of mist,

that at times masks
the mystery of syncopation.

Beneath this, I am reggae, blues, jazz,
funk, rock, folk.

Even when I miss a downbeat
or let inaudible chords fly
free like an improv magician,

I have never stopped dancing
to the steps of love
you have freely given me.

So, I remain the one who
slips on the staircase of
syncopation, sliding

up and down, in and out
and all around at once—

a crow in free fall.

Love (at last) Entered

This morning as the sun
arose steaming above winter's
crisp landscape, love entered

the scene and everything
in that instant, *transformed*.

Where hopelessness had lain
suspended in time, hope leaped up
and began dancing, as if she knew

each of the steps necessary
to express such love.

Let *this* love enter the marrow
of your life, and be simply amazed
at whom you truly are,

revealed anew—
upon the canvas
of your own life.

About the Author

Paul Goldman is an Ecstatic Poet who lives and breathes these words of ecstasy sourced from his Divine. After undergoing open-heart surgery in January of 2014, Paul now is more than ever engaged on a passionate mission to spread these messages of peace, solace and connection to something greater than one's human self.

Paul produced the Spoken Word CD *Wild Joy Released: The Ecstatic Poetry of Paul Goldman* with the assistance of friend and extraordinary musician Tom Jacobs. Just a few short months later, *Wild Joy: Ruminations* was published in 2010 by River Sanctuary Publishing. In praising this ecstatic volume, one reviewer compared the poems to Rumi:

> ...The wild, holy energy within this book can burst forth only from a 'man who has lost himself in love', such as Rumi and other seers, whose poetry this volume now joins.
>
> Vern Barnet, Faiths and Beliefs columnist, The Kansas City Star

In 2011, renowned publisher, O-Books of London, England published Paul's second collection of ecstatic poetry, *Journey Into Oneness*. Of this work, Melissa Studdard, MFA, Contributing Editor Tiferet and award-winning author of Six Weeks to Yehida, said:

> ...This is not just a book. It is a metaphysical experience.

Paul is the former host of *Journey Into Oneness* on Co-Creator Radio Network, founder of Gratitude Open Mic Night, past proprietor of Stone Spirit Lodge – a Metaphysical Shoppe and most recently he has become a regular contributor to James Van Praagh's blog, *The Daily Awakening*.

Find out more about Paul Goldman at
    www.ecstaticpoet.com

Follow him on Twitter @SpiritPoet and at his Facebook page, Wild Joy: The Ecstatic Poetry of Paul Goldman.

About the Artist

Natosha Keefer considers herself an inspirational artist. Working *sans* shoes and accompanied by music, she enters into a visual dialogue with her canvas as her brush dances across it. The addition of burlap, sand, and other materials gives added dimension to each unique work. She often creates her art before an audience. Natosha believes her art to be not only a  reflection of her authentic self, but that it is in part a product of the creative synergy which results from her interaction with those sharing her experience.

Natosha's art background extends far beyond painting – she is also an accomplished dancer and musician.
Find out even more about this gifted visionary artist at
    www.natoshakeefer.com

PAINTINGS by Natosha Keefer

p.1 – *Upon Your Canvas*

p.8 – *Another Starry Night*

p.27 – *By Your Still Waters*

p.32 – *Reaching Out*

p.49 – *Deeper*

p.59 – *Dancing in the Shift*

p.62 – *(Untitled)*